THE
LOG HOME

Classic Log Cabins of North America

by Nancy L. Mohr

RUNNING PRESS
PHILADELPHIA · LONDON

Credits

© Accent Alaska/Ken Graham Agency:

Ken Graham: pp. 3 (top), 21, 32–33, 59, 60, 62

Rolf Hicker: p. 14

Chad Case: p. 36 (top)

Dicon Joseph: p 64–65

Dan Perkins/Cross Fox Photography: p. 71 (background)

Steven Seiller: p. 74

© Aiuppy Photographs: pp. 42 (top), 49

© Theo Allofs: Front cover, pp. 8, 12–13, 31

© Barrett & Mackay Photography Inc.: p. 30

© Corbis:

Joseph Sohm: p. 9 (top)

Peter Johnson: p. 16

Kevin R. Morris: pp. 18, 22 (bottom)

Michael Freeman: p. 22 (top)

Patrick W. Stoll: p. 26

Michael T. Sedam: p. 3 (bottom), 52

Layne Kennedy: p. 66

Ric Ergenbright: pp. 78–79

George Lepp: p. 80

© Jeff Gnass Photography: pp. 4, 5 (background), 27 (background), 38, 40, 48, 50, 70

© Jim Hargan. pp. 6, 15, 36 (bottom), 37, 44, 45 (background), 46, 75

© Grant Heilman Photography, Inc.:

Larry LeFever: Back cover, pp. 43, 69

Runk/Schoenberger: p. 1

© The Image Finders:

Jim Baron: p. 28

© Don Pitcher: pp. 20, 24, 25, 53 (background), 54, 56–57, 76

© James P. Rowan Photography: pp. 7, 9 (bottom), 19 (background), 39 (background), 42 (bottom), 58, 72

© Gary Schultz: pp. 10, 61 (background), 63

© Kurt Thorson: p. 68

© 2001 by Running Press

Printed in China

9 8 7 6 5 4 3 2

Digit on the right indicates the number of this printing

Library of Congress Cataloging-in-Publication Number 2001087015

ISBN 0-7624-1117-1

Text written by Nancy Mohr
Designed by Gwen Galeone
Edited by Victoria Hyun
Typography: Adobe Garamond and Poetica

This book may be ordered by mail from the publisher. **But try your bookstore first!**

Published by Courage Books, an imprint of
Running Press Book Publishers
125 South Twenty-second Street
Philadelphia, Pennsylvania 19103-4399

Visit us on the web!
www.runningpress.com

Previous page: *Noah "Bud" Ogle log cabin, built 1879* **(Opposite page) Top:** *Kantishna Roadhouse, Alaska* **Bottom:** *Old log cabin in Antelope Flats with the Grand Teton Mountains as a backdrop, Grand Teton National Park, Wyoming*

Contents

CHAPTER 1

The Quest

O n a high shelf rests a well worn, falling apart book worth handling gently. It belonged to a boy who received it as a Christmas gift in 1913. Within its pages is the story of Rolf, a fifteen-year-old orphan who ran away from abusive relatives in the early 1800s and found refuge with a kindly Indian who taught him how to live off the land. It wasn't the sort of book that was supposed to be interesting to a little girl, but when it was handed down to me I dreamed of building a cabin like Rolf's:

"I suppose every trapper that ever lived, on first building a cabin, said, 'Oh, any little thing will do, so long as it has a roof and is big enough to lie down in.' And every trapper has realized before spring that he made a sad mistake in not having it big enough to live in and store goods in. Quonab and Rolf were new at the business, and made the usual mistake. They planned their cabin far too small; 10 x 12 feet, instead of 12 x 20 feet they made it, and 6 feet walls, instead of 8 feet walls. Both were expert axemen. Spruce was plentiful and the cabin rose quickly. In one day the walls were up. An important thing was the roof. What should it be? Overlapping basswood troughs, split shingles, also called shakes, or clay? By far the easiest

Left: *Puckett cabin and snake rail fence, Blue Ridge Parkway, Virginia* **This page:** *A log cache frames distant Wrangell Mountains in autumn, Lee Westenburg Visitor Center, Tetlin National Wildlife Refuge, Alaska*

Above: *Interior of a furnished log tavern circa 1800, located in the Crockett Tavern Museum, Hamblen County, Tennessee*

Right: *Polperro House, a Pendervis State Historic Site, Mineral Point, Wisconsin*

to make, the warmest in the winter and coolest in the summer, is the clay roof. It has three disadvantages: It leaks in long-continued wet weather; it drops down dust and dirt in dry weather; and is so heavy that it usually ends up crushing in the log rafters and beams, unless they are further supported on posts, which are much in the way. But its advantages were so obvious that the builders did not hesitate. A clay roof it was to be.

When the walls were 5 feet high, the doorway and window were cut through the logs, but leaving in each case one half of the log at the bottom of the needed opening. The top log was now placed, then rolled over bottom up, while half of its thickness was cut away to fit over the door: a similar cut was made over the window. Two flat pieces of spruce were prepared for the door jambs and two shorter ones for window jambs. Auger holes were put through, so as to allow an oak pin to be driven through the jamb into each log, and the doorway and window opening were done.

The eaves logs, end logs, and ridge logs were soon in place; then came the cutting of small poles, spruce and tamarack, long

Top: *Log structure that housed George Washington's soldiers during the American Revolution at Valley Forge, Pennsylvania* **Bottom:** *French log cabin, Fort Michilmackinac, Mackinac City, Michigan* **Left:** *Small log cabin and rainbow in the Kluane Range, Yukon, Canada*

Above: *S led dogs and sled*
at Wolf Run Cabin at sunrise

Overleaf: *A log cabin winters*
in Yukon, Canada

enough to reach from ridge to eaves, and in sufficient number to completely cover the roof. A rank sedge meadow near by afforded plenty of
coarse grass with which the poles were covered deeply; and lastly clay dug
out with a couple of hand-made, axe-hewn wooden spades was thrown
evenly on the grass to a depth of 6 inches; this, when trampled flat, made
a roof that served them well.

The chinks of the logs when large were filled with split pieces of
wood; when small they were plugged with moss. A door was made of
hewn planks, and hinged very simply on two pins; one made by letting
the plank project as a point, the other by nailing on a pin after the door
was placed; both pins fitting, of course, into inch auger holes.

It had a sweet fragrance of wood and moss, and the pleasure it gave
to Rolf at least was something he never again could expect to find in
equal measure about any other dwelling he might make."

Ernest Thompson Seton, *Rolf in the Woods,* 1911

Ninety years after Rolf's cabin was created in a writer's imagination, it lingers in mine—a childhood memory, a fantasy all grown up. I suspect nearly everyone has some degree of affection for log cabins, however imperfect the underlying knowledge may be. The "where" and "how" isn't important—whether from direct experience or the pages of a book, perhaps from elderly relatives' stories of "the olden days" or as a child spending happy hours playing with Lincoln logs. Log cabin legends have strengthened the idea of log construction as being intensely American, an enduring symbol of pioneer spirit and self-sufficiency—even though it is generally accepted that the building technique originated in northern Europe. Without this relatively simple, durable form of do-it-yourself housing, the pioneers might never have ventured beyond the first range of mountains.

Log cabins have never lost their allure. They are especially appealing as the subject of historical study. Most of those who embark upon a serious search for log homes complete the task many thousands of miles later. There is always one more to be found, to be photographed, sketched, and catalogued before it disappears before the onslaught of "progress." Determination of the historic or practical value of a log cabin may be less than objective: one man's cabin may be another's castle.

The best hunting ground is along old travel routes—Indian trails that became horse trails, then rutted wagon roads, and eventually paved highways. The turnpikes and interstate highways are too sterile as they fling themselves through one state after another, barely touching on communities past or present. However, many of the log buildings along the more historic routes began as pony express stations and early post offices, with some expanding into rudimentary inns for weary travelers. Not all of them are immediately recognizable as log construction. As owners prospered, and uses changed, the logs were often covered with planks or clapboard siding and the interior walls plastered. It isn't unusual to find the remnants of a log cabin deep in the heart of a frame or stone house. When our architect son was working on the restoration of an old farmhouse only half a mile from where we live, he discovered that most of the house was an early nineteenth century plank house—hewn planks with chinking

between, completely covered with plaster inside and stucco outside. The planks went only to the bottom of the second floor level, indicating that the house was originally a single story with the roof raised at a later date. Exposing the interior surface of the planks added warmth and a sense of history. The next owner wanted more space, moved the old house to the center of the property and enveloped it in new construction, still preserving the plank section for its historic value.

Above: The window of an old Alaskan log cabin peeks out in Brooks Range, Alaska

Right: The cozy atmosphere of a log cabin's front porch is evident in the Western Mountain region of Transylvania County

Far-flung sources of intriguing, often well-preserved log cabins offer a range from the small crib-type to buildings of substantial size—with or without stone, frame, or brick additions. Pennsylvania, because of its natural access to the lands across the Ohio River, was and still is dotted with uncountable numbers of log cabins. The old Lincoln Highway (Route 30) running from Philadelphia to Pittsburgh passes through dozens of small towns where log cabins still stand. From Uniontown, Pennsylvania to Hagerstown, Maryland along Route 40, log cabins hide beneath a considerable number of the clapboard-sided houses. As late as 1967, twenty-three log houses, five barns and a church clung to the side of a mountain in Fayette County, Pennsylvania. The diligent treasure hunter will find pioneer cabins in Missouri between Moberly and Jefferson City. Dayton,

Ohio's first log structure, built in 1796, survives as the Newcomb Log Tavern, which at various times has been a tavern, home, courthouse, school, church, post office and is now a tourist attraction. In Weaversville, North Carolina, a restored pine cabin serves as a memorial to Zebulon B. Vance who served the state in Congress and as governor. About three times as large as a typical mountain cabin, it was once considered a showplace. The well-known song, "Home on the Range" was written in a log cabin in Smith Center, Kansas. Clearly, log cabins have provided an appropriate environment for a virtually endless range of activities.

In Jackson, Wyoming and nearby Jackson Hole, the long history of log house construction is still evolving. Lodgepole pines flourish there, growing as dense stands of very tall, straight trees. Uniform in size with few branches, they provide logs for construction. The strange shapes that the occasionally diseased trees develop are a bonus since they can be worked into stair railings or unusual supports for picnic shelters or porches.

In the 1800s, entire towns were built near the lodgepole forests to house workers who were hired to make railroad ties and became known as "tie hacks." This was totally different work from felling trees for log cabins. The ties had to be hewn to precise dimensions to support the ambitious railroad expansion.

The quality of the early log cabins reflects the skills of the individual builders, some of whom learned to use an axe on the spot. The work was hard and often dangerous. However, survival was sufficient motivation for any settler, especially one whose responsibilities included wife and children.

Although logs like any other wood are subject to decay, the best preserved cabins are those that have never been abandoned, have perhaps experienced changes in use that encouraged good maintenance, or have a history important enough for them to be carefully restored as memorials to a person or event. The history of log construction reaches back to the very beginning of this country—to the first settlements on the North American continent—and new chapters are still being written.

Left: *A guest log cabin in Katchemak Bay near Homer, Alaska*

CHAPTER 2

New World: First Generation

Log cabins are good examples of folk architecture. They serve as a physical record of the people who cut the trees, prepared the logs and built these serviceable dwellings. The first log cabins were paid for with courage and hard work as primary currency. It wasn't easy to prepare each log and heave it into place, even with the rare luxury of having others to help.

Log Cabins originally appeared in the Delaware Valley, which can be defined as eastern Pennsylvania, southwestern New Jersey and northern Delaware. The Swedes and Finns were probably the first settlers to imprint log cabin design on the new territory, transferring their skills in building with notched logs from central and northern Europe. Settlers from other cultures adopted these basic forms, developing floor plans that can be traced back to British and Scotch-Irish immigrants. The Germans, too, were active in log construction, employing slightly different styles that depended upon whether they came from the eastern or alpine sections of Germany. Far from the main concentrations of settlers and even earlier, Russian influence was strong in Alaska's log cabins which were more elegant than those in the pioneer communities. The corner notching was unique, and the designs were often elaborate.

Left: *Log cabins and wagons in Old Trail Town, a ghost town in Cody, Wyoming* **This page:** *Log farm house, Westfield Heritage Village, Cambridge, Ontario, Canada*

Above: *M*oose

antlers, Eagle, Alaska

Right: *An old timer's cabin*

with rusting tools in Alaska

In Canada, Frenchmen settled in what is today Quebec where log cabins took on a different appearance. They were built with vertical logs instead of the more familiar horizontal pattern. The vertical style tracked historically to France, especially Normandy. It was certainly easier to work with the shorter, vertical logs than to lift longer logs into horizontal position. A vertical log house could be built more quickly, by fewer people. In other areas of the continent, the vertical option was frequently seen in stockade and other fortification construction.

Log construction wasn't favored by every group of settlers. The English applied their energies to splitting timbers for clapboards, and building houses like those they left behind in England. However, the widespread popularity of log homes was illustrated as recently as 1951, with a count of 10,000 to 12,000 old log houses in Georgia alone in the form of courthouses, jails, forts, and churches. And, of course, legend has it that Daniel Boone left a succession of log cabins behind him as he led the way from Pennsylvania to Virginia and on to North Carolina. If a set-

Top: *Reconstruction of Whig Party headquarters circa 1840* **Bottom:** *Shadows fall across the porch of a log cabin in Old Trail Town, in Cody, Wyoming*

tler planned to stay where he was, a frame house may have been appropriate. If he was on the move, exploring new territory, the log cabin was his choice.

The term "log cabin" referred most often to a primitive, one room style of house. It didn't take long for the crude cabin to be supplanted by log houses which might have more doors, windows, a central fireplace, additional rooms—the amenities depending upon the skill and material wealth of the owner. The settlers showed individuality in their decisions about placement of a fireplace or the design of a dwelling where two fireplaces were desired. For instance, a central fireplace might warm two rooms, one large room in front and, minimally, a smaller one behind the main room. Two log cabins with a breezeway between and a fireplace in each outside wall were known as a "double den." Two double dens provided more space and privacy, with four units and four breezeways. "Saddle bag" is a good descriptive name for two units—usually of the same size—connected by a central fireplace. Gable end fireplaces served a single room and often had exterior chimneys. A cabin with a corner fireplace was evidence of Swedish influence. Without doubt, cabin and farm were a settler's most tangible evidence of accomplishment.

As settlers moved away from the more populated coastal areas, the initial westward expansion went only as far as the mountains of Pennsylvania—around 1730 and on into the 1750s. By 1758, they were across the Ohio River. Ultimately, for each new cabin, the choices were tempered by practicality and available raw materials.

The most primitive log cabins, barns and outbuildings were built of round logs, and were generally seen in the mountains and among certain Indian tribes. These were crude structures with random spacing between the logs, unless the builder was fortunate enough to find very regular limbs that would fit evenly on top of one another. As settlers became more skilled with their axes, they worked the logs so that they could fit tightly, or intentionally left spaces when they fit the corners to allow for chinking. The wall height usually depended upon number of men available to lift, lever and push. When sawmills moved into a particular area, the more prosperous settlers often purchased board siding to hide the logs.

Above: *South Pass State Historic Site in South Pass, Wyoming*

Right: *Remains of an old log cabin, Billy Wells Dude Ranch, Pinedale, Wyoming*

In time, cabin builders learned to be selective about their choice of wood. White oak was the best for cabins although poplar was strong and became stronger as it aged. The hardwoods like cherry and walnut were reserved for furniture, while hickory could be depended upon to burn hot and virtually smokeless in the fireplace.

The structure of the corners determined the strength of the house, preventing sideways slippage and carrying the combined weight of two walls joining. There were plenty of choices in making sure the corner connections were strong—V-notches, saddle notches, tongue-and-groove, butt joints, halved cornering, and probably endless adaptations that suited circumstances and materials. The undersided notch was the most common, a thoroughly practical choice that didn't collect rainwater—preventing rot and decay. A V-notch is similar to an undersided notch. Alternatives included the oversided notch, double saddle notch, full dovetail, half-dovetail, square notch, half notch and, rather unusual, diamond notching.

Log cabins east of the Mississippi were a product of the urge to move west "for land, gold and glory," as a writer of the time commented. The cabins represented temporary, even emergency shelter more than expression of a preference. Second generation homes in the same area were more likely to be built of sawn lumber. It probably appeared that the log cabin era was ending.

CHAPTER 3

And Then . . .

It was the early 20th century, and log cabin romance appeared upon the scene. Log cabins were no longer necessary, but had risen to the realm of the nostalgic. With turn of the century fortunes to spend, the Great Camps of the Adirondacks took shape. Architect-designed, large, and well built with every possible amenity included, local carpenters and masons had more work than they ever dreamed of, producing main lodges, guest quarters, servants' quarters, dining halls, boathouses, and workshops—all of log construction. Utility gave way to rustic elegance. An element as basic as caulking might be replaced with carefully scribed and painted boards to fit between the logs—to fool the eye, so the casual observer would think it was mortar. Well-heeled New Yorkers and Philadelphians traveled long hours by train and automobile to delude themselves into believing they were living the simple life for a few weeks each summer. And, surely, nothing was omitted from the supplies that contributed to their comfort.

Log construction soared in popularity for all sorts of private hideaways, hunting retreats and, not surprisingly, National Park lodges. Yellowstone National Park's Old Faithful Inn was one of the more dramatic examples, built in 1904 with an eight-story lobby, 140

Left: *A good example of a modern log home* **This page:** *Logs and construction detail on the Rhodes cabin, Great Basin National Park, Nevada*

Above: *View of an interior of a modern log home. Note the exposed beams and stone fireplace*

rooms, three sets of balconies, a widow's walk and a crow's nest. A number of corporate hideaways were rather impressive, too. In Montana, Anaconda Copper's success inspired the CEO to commission fourteen log and stone buildings for corporate retreats and the entertainment of business and personal friends. With the depression and then World War II, the less solvent of these mammoth estates—hardly "ranches"—fell into disrepair and have since been reclaimed as upscale guest ranches. The remnants of the elegant log era exhibit the addition of shutters, partial siding, dormers, new roof lines and interesting manifestations of simple and ornate adaptations to basic log construction—the result being an expression of the owner's personal concept of style, all the way from folksy to funky to modern.

My personal affection for log cabins dates back to childhood and the family cabin a couple of hours north of New York City. Compared to homes in the Westchester County suburb where we lived, the cabin was pretty rustic, built in the late 1930s of peeled logs, intended to appeal as a weekend getaway. Well removed from a narrow dirt road, it perched on a hillside clearing in a birch grove carpeted with lush ferns, ground pine and velvet mosses. With Dutch doors at the entry and also from the kitchen to a covered porch where meals were served around a big rustic table in warm weather, it was indeed a total change from home. Everyone relaxed, forgot about rushing around and didn't mind if all the silver and cups and saucers didn't match. French doors leading from the living room onto the same porch were flung open in all but the worst weather. A large stone fireplace with floor to ceiling bookshelves on either side claimed most of the longest wall—bracketed by window seats that filled a dual role as extra bunks. I loved winter weekends when I could burrow under a pile of quilts and drift off to sleep watching the firelight flicker on the beamed ceiling. Two bedrooms and a bath completed the room count. Overstuffed wing chairs were for curling up with books. Cannel coal (hot fire, lots of light) was the fuel of choice in the fireplace—the only source of heat in cold weather. A short distance through the woods, a blue agate cup hung on a tree by a bubbling, clear spring: the water was so cold it almost took your breath away. No matter how long a stay at the cabin, it was always too soon to pack to go home.

The cabins of my college years, belonged to a classmate's family—deep in the forests of northeastern Pennsylvania at the edge of a large man-made lake. Built in the roaring '20s, they had harbored expansive house parties, watched sailboats sink to the bottom when the wealthy owners failed to pull them out before winter ice set in, and weathered the depression. They came into their own again as the next generation went off to college in the 1950s. This was a heavenly retreat for an occasional off-campus weekend, complete with roaring fires, huge quantities of hamburgers, spaghetti, and ice cream—a toss of the coin to see who rated the main cabin's master bedroom, cleverly hidden behind a swinging bookcase. The other guests snuggled under Hudson Bay blankets on the window seats and couches, and the men of the moment were relegated to built-in bunks in the sprawling second floor loft. Even a rainy day wasn't hard to take, for the floor to ceiling shelves were crammed with books to suit

Above: *Log cabin along Goose Bay in Labrador, Newfoundland, Canada*

Opposite Page: *Log home with deck shrouded in mist*

every taste, spirited ping-pong games were for the asking, and there was always plenty of talk, talk, talk.

Large or small, these were log cabins at their recreational best, a far cry from the cabins that sheltered the waves of pioneers following the shifting frontier westward. Another chapter of cabin fever was launched by the government during the Depression when agencies were established to create jobs for the unemployed: the Works Progress Administration (WPA), and the

Overleaf: $\mathcal{T}$*his*

beautiful log cabin sits in the

Glacier Valley at the base

of Mount Alyeska ski resort

in Alaska

Above: *The interior of*

Sportsman's Lodge, French

River, Prince Edward Island,

Canada

Civilian Conservation Corps (CCC). Working with the U.S. Forest Service and the National Park Service, literally thousands of log buildings—lookout towers, ranger stations, lodges, bridges—were constructed. Visitors to the parks saw visible evidence of their tax dollars in use. Museums built reproductions of historic log structures although the log village museum in Cody, Wyoming is for real. These log buildings were disassembled at their original sites, moved and reassembled to inform visitors about the way the West grew and housed its people. The collection runs from a crude log home built for General Custer's scout to an in-town building with a high false front just like the ones in Western movies.

Fascination with log cabins lingers even when busy days leave little or no time to do-it-yourself, and certainly not with crude tools or measurements of "10 by 7" meaning axe handles rather than feet. A request on the Internet for information about "log cabins" will generate a listing of some 240 web sites ranging from custom builders to pre-builders to prefabricated packages and historic preservation. Although the available cabins fit any taste and budget, the basic form and components haven't changed. This is truly the indigenous American architecture. The durable log cabin surfaces as mountain lodges, summer camps for fishing and hunting, road side inns, and rest stops—and in more recent years, once again as year-round homes. Americans have never stopped building log cabins, and probably never will.

An isolated cabin fills the need to be alone in a society where privacy has eroded dramatically. Hopefully, it is a place where it is possible to escape, if only momentarily, from a pace that pioneers could not have imagined in their wildest dreams. Think about electronic everything—credit ratings, financial and personal information that are only too public, and then traffic jams, lines at the airport, endless telephone minutes on "hold." Solitude is wonderful—and rare. Sometimes we don't know what to do with it when we have it, but maybe it would be nice to try a log cabin.

Americans, perhaps even more today than before, view log cabins as an icon of "good and admirable." The historic reality was certainly less than glamorous. Try to imagine a small, crowded cabin where the whole family slept, ate, worked, played, bred, and was frequently joined by travelers in need (some of them legitimately in need of assistance, others looking to take advantage of a settler's kindness and occasionally to even steal his meager possessions). Open fireplaces were a hazard for the sparks they threw and the potential for injuring children playing or sleeping near the hearth. Primitive sanitary facilities meant a trip outside in all kinds of weather, and keeping the fire stoked was a never-ending task. When the clay caulk crumbled, cold winds blew through the cracks. Snow sifted in and settled on the dirt floor, warmth from the fire melted it, and there you were slipping around in mucky indoor mud. Ventilation was generally non-existent, too hot or too cold, guaranteed to produce a mix of good and not-so-good odors.

Top: *Cabin bedecked in Christmas lights in Girdwood, Alaska* **Bottom:** *An interesting entrance into a modern dining room in Jackson County, North Carolina* **Right:** *A glimpse inside the Mast Farm Inn Bed and Breakfast in Watauga County, Boone Area, Valle Crucis, North Carolina*

CHAPTER 4

Log Cabins & Political Correctness

The persistence of many log cabin myths must reside with the early creators of national political campaigns. Looking for ways to make a candidate seem more honest, more sincere, more capable of holding the highest office in the land, someone happened upon the log cabin as a symbol—leading to the (somewhat tentative) confirmation of eight presidents as having been born in log cabins. It became beneficial if not eminently advisable for candidates to be born in log cabins which naturally led to controversy of this or that state's, county's, town's claim to fame.

Major debate arose over Andrew Jackson's place of birth, with both North and South Carolina claiming him for his log cabin birth. The argument was never settled to either state's satisfaction. Apparently, his parents built a house in North Carolina but his father died before he was born. His mother went to live with one of her two sisters, one living in North Carolina and the other in South Carolina. There seems to be an absence of records about which state can legitimately claim Jackson as a favorite son. The argument lasted long after the death of Jackson himself which is not surprising since he was a rather contentious person

Left: *The log cabin in which Abraham Lincoln was born, located now at the Abraham Lincoln Birthplace National Historic Site, Hodgenville, Kentucky* **This page:** *Brotherton cabin in Chickamanga Battlefield, Fort Oglethorpe, Georgia*

Above: *This
log cabin is the site of
Booker T. Washington's
birth, Booker T. Washington
National Monument,
Virginia*

anyway. There are memorials to him in both states. If he was indeed born
in a log cabin, he may have preceded the generally accepted first log cabin
president, William Henry Harrison. Clever campaign managers had not
yet surfaced when Jackson ran for president, so the question of birth in a
log cabin showed little or no potential for being a political bonus. Lucky
North Carolina had another chance to register a log cabin president in
James Knox Polk.

President James Buchanan acquired his log cabin label by accident.
After escaping a house fire, his family took refuge in a cabin where,
apparently, he was born. It made his constituents happy to think of a log
cabin birth, so no objection was made. The supposed birthplace has been
dissembled a couple of times, moved from its original site in Mercersburg,
Pennsylvania to nearby Chambersburg and then to the grounds of
Mercersburg Academy. The question asked but never answered: Was the
right one moved? Actually, the log cabin did not play an important part

in his political history until after his death when Pennsylvanians wanted to make the point that they had a log cabin president, too.

Without doubt, Abraham Lincoln was the best known log cabin president. Major emphasis was placed on his simple roots before and after his election. The cabin theme was pure showmanship for those who came after, and even for Lincoln there can be no certainty that references to "the traditional birthplace cabin" correctly target The Cabin. Since the family did a lot of moving around, claims to the Lincoln's cabin have been made over the years by Kentucky, Indiana, and Illinois. Maybe they are all right. Lincoln did live in more than one log cabin.

It is possible that Andrew Johnson was born in a log cabin; he is included among "the eight." Ulysses S. Grant lived in a cabin home, but most likely not built of logs. James A. Garfield is another uncertain cabin dweller, but perhaps the most widely publicized. The wholesome quality of the birthplaces of Harrison, Lincoln, and Garfield did not provide them with any special personal protection for they were all three the victims of assassination.

Teddy Roosevelt's vision for parkland preservation resulted in the establishment of the country's first wilderness preserve, Yellowstone National Park. He was a natural for inclusion in log cabin lore although his upbringing in New York City did not include birth in a cabin. Roosevelt acquired a ranch in the Dakota Territory at the age of twenty-five. Two of his ranchers collected heavy ponderosa pine logs that had floated down the river, snagged on sandbars and the bank. They built a cabin for him. The logs were already hand-hewn, originally cut far upstream for railroad ties. After he became President, the cabin was dismantled several times for display, and eventually the legend evolved that this was the cabin where he was born. All legend, no substance.

In spite of the romantic stories that eddied about the log cabin, they were no guarantee that the log cabin environment produced either honesty or a high ethical standard. John Wilkes Booth and Jesse James, among others, were born in log cabins.

Top: *Theodore Roosevelt's Log Cabin, "Maltese Cross" Ranch Cabin, Theodore Roosevelt National Park, North Dakota*
Bottom: *Commander-in-Chief's guard huts, Valley Forge, Pennsylvania*   **Right:** *Soldier huts on the original street of Muhlenberg's Brigade, Valley Forge National Park, Valley Forge, Pennsylvania*

CHAPTER 5

Design & Construction: Old

The young country's version of the mobile family of the 18th century built uncountable log cabins with few decent tools and minimal skills, producing them in response to urgent need. The necessary skills were not part of the "new world package." The immigrants learned on the job. Whether woodsman, hunter or family man, severe winters demanded adequate shelter, accounting for the emergence of log cabins in frontier Pennsylvania and in the mountains of Maryland and Virginia. Log construction, no matter how crude, provided security of a sort that would resist attacks with arrows and bullets by Indians or bandits. After an attack was driven off, settlers would salvage lead bullets that had lodged in the logs, melt and remold them—recycling at its most basic. Families built in clusters for safety, building stockades when they could, creating crude miniatures of the European walled cities they left behind.

These sturdy frontier people had no nails or spikes to use in building and usually only a single tool—an axe. Without a good axe, there was no means of felling trees, clearing land, cutting wood for fuel, and fencing in livestock. The axes that the colonists carried from Europe were patterned after a Roman design—with some influence from European war axes.

Left: *Interior of Tatum Cabin, circa 1785, Hickory Ridge Homestead Museum, North Carolina* **This page:** *A spinning wheel in a log farmhouse, Oconaluftee Pioneer Farmstead, Great Smoky Mountains National Park, North Carolina*

Above: *An*

abandoned log cabin near

Whittier, North Carolina

By 1740, the axe had been improved for heavier American frontier use—with the surface opposite the blade designed as a multi-purpose sledge for pounding fence posts into the ground, or splitting rocks. Most frontier woodsmen guarded their axes carefully, making and substituting heavy wooden mauls or sledges for pounding and splitting.

The expert woodsman who used his axe to the greatest advantage was, in the opinion of Richard Lillard, writing in The Great Forest, "equivalent in artistry to a bow in the hands of a great violinist." A master axeman knew how to judge a tree and what could be done with it—with similarity to a sculptor looking deep into the heart of a block of stone to discover the form he would release. The woodsman placed his wedges just right, avoided troublesome knots, and hit a log at exactly the right angle. In felling a tree, he made two opposing cuts, one a little lower than another so that the tree would fall exactly where he wanted it to go. Each task was completed with great energy and a certain rhythm.

The siting of a cabin was important. There was fairly universal agreement about facing east to enjoy the early morning sun, finding shelter from the wind near the bottom of a hill but not where a heavy rain might flood a cabin, being near a spring or running stream and not far from a good source of firewood. Cabins were built and then left behind if the water supply failed or there was no more firewood.

A good logger choose and cut trees of the same species and diameter so that walls would be relatively even in height and width. Retention of the bark on round logs protected against decay. Sometimes he used his axe to hew the top and bottom surfaces so they would fit together more smoothly. Hauling logs to the site was heavy work alone or even with his wife and children. As settlements grew, log raising joined barn raising as a communal effort. A group of neighbors cutting, raising, and then chinking the spaces between logs with mud could build a fairly substantial cabin far more quickly than the most energetic solitary settler and his family.

The first four logs were used as a foundation, or laid on top of foundation stones. Notched joists were fitted into them to support the floor—assuming there would be a plank or half log floor. Wall logs were laid one on top of another, going around the perimeter of the cabin to raise the walls evenly and fitting them together with notches at the corners—where each new course of logs held the previous one in place with its weight.

If the builder was fortunate enough to own other tools, a neater cabin might be the result. Sometimes the ends of random length logs stuck out, but real craftsmen made sure they were cut off evenly. Two limbs at either end of the cabin wall were set diagonally to hold the ridgepole. Additional limbs formed the roof skeleton which was then covered with tree limbs or shakes. Spaces between the roofing materials were filled with moss, mud, smaller pieces of wood, and stones. When available, animal skins were hung on the walls for insulation.

The language of wood cutting made good sense. A log was a whole timber. A half timber was a log that had been sliced in half and then the round sides squared off. A whole

Above: *Rabbitbrush and sheepherder's log line shack, Dinosaur National Monument, Colorado*

Right: *Log cabin detail at Chimney Rock National Historic Site, Nebraska*

log hewn square but used in horizontal notched construction is still called a log. Hewn logs generally produce a tighter fit although the final product was a matter of the builder's skill. Corner notching is usually different on round or hewn logs. If cut to be smaller than a half timber—then it is called a plank, and the house becomes a plank house. This can be confusing since a house of unnotched planks nailed to studding is also a plank house. Noah Webster generated some more confusion with the 1828 edition of his dictionary where he states that a log is a log only if it is used in constructing a log hut.

And then there are the details. A typical front door (often the only door) was made of heavy wood slabs fastened together with pegs and opened outward to allow more room in the cabin. Hinges were made of

Above: *H̶ornbeck*

Homestead circa 1870,

Florissant Fossil Beds National

Monument, Colorado

wood or animal skin and were mounted on the inside. A wood latch or crossbar served as a lock. Attached to the latch and threaded through a hole in the door, a string of buckskin hung outside. At night, the string was pulled inside for security. The latchstring hanging outside became a symbol of hospitality—an invitation for a well intentioned stranger to enter. Frontier settlers were remarkably hospitable, a characteristic that didn't necessarily come from Europe. It's possible that the common experiences and challenges made them more receptive to the idea of helping others.

A better cabin might enjoy smoothed floor boards and a large, well-built fireplace, although it might have initially had a dirt floor followed by a puncheon floor in which logs were split lengthwise and laid on the ground with flat sides up.

Often structural differences could be categorized by region. Windows were rare although substitutes were created with animal skins or sliding boards. Eventually, paper greased with animal fat for waterproofing and translucency provided limited light. Window glass was not manufactured in America until the 1800s, and even then it was expensive and fragile. Walls were built without windows, but windows could be cut out at a later date.

An open loft frequently served as children's sleeping quarters or for storage, accessible with a a ladder of tree limbs or pegs stuck in walls. The loft was also a place for drying herbs, apples, and peppers and storing non-perishable foods. Not every cabin had a loft. More often, the entire family lived in the single common room.

Fireplaces were important for heat and cooking, and are still a "vestigial cultural trait." Most people enjoy the warmth and cheery glow of a fireplace, even if heating isn't a priority. A pioneering family huddled around the fire for warmth on a bitterly cold winter day. Anyone who has experienced dependence on a fireplace knows that the heat is highly localized, and that leaving the immediate vicinity results in rapid cooling.

Most cabins were raised in a hurry. Each one was as different as the natural building materials that were available. It was an intense schedule of cut the trees, trim the logs, drag them to the house site, cut the notches, get the logs up. If there were three or more workers, all the better. A single person could build a small cabin, but he was limited by the height to which he could raise the logs—and those would be short logs. With more help, the use of longer logs was possible, and the builders could use skids and ropes to guide logs into place. While a cabin was being built, families would live in a lean-to made of tree boughs, a makeshift tent, in or under their wagon.

A family's first log cabin was often intended as a temporary shelter, but as more babies came along, and money was scarce, a larger house was not always possible. The little cabin nurtured strong family bonds, and that family was an independent, self-sustaining, producing, and consuming social unit. Although many of the early settlers were ill prepared in terms of skills, they hardly lacked for determination. Log cabins represented security; you knew that if logs were available, you could provide for your family.

CHAPTER 6

Past . . .

An old log house writes its history in three dimensional form. Some of the chapters are easy to read. Others leave the most experienced translator scratching his (or her) head. As is the case with historic farmhouses, the best cabins are those where the owners did not have enough wealth to "modernize" along the way.

Along a once-country road in West Grove, Pennsylvania, a log house with brick and stone wings is in the process of being reborn. The new owners purchased the house with a surrounding four acres. Originally, it was part of a larger property where the farmer still keeps dairy cows in a nearby barn. It is cause for great amusement that as soon as the cows in the pasture hear the sound of the farmer's pickup truck on the gravel road, they head straight for the barn. And, yes, the barn could probably tell some stories, too.

The log section of the house was built somewhere between 1722 and 1735. The logs are massive 12 feet chestnut logs—hewn on the outside and inside surfaces, but left round top and bottom. Each log sits directly upon the one below with the corners stabilized with dove-tailing. The tight fit left little or no room for chinking. What chinking there is from the con-

Left: *Old log cabin in Antelope Flats with the Grand Teton Mountains as a backdrop, Grand Teton National Park, Wyoming* **This page:** *An old cabin in Livengood, Alaska*

Above: *O*ld *homestead north of Fort Laramie, Wyoming*

Overleaf: *Old Anna Schmitgen homestead buildings (Diamond Bar Ranch) near Devils Tower, Wyoming*

tact area to the side surfaces is mud with perhaps some straw or horsehair in the mix. Over the years, the logs—green when cut—experienced normal shrinking, displacing some of the chinking and slowly changing the alignment of the walls. The relatively good condition of the logs in 2001 can be explained by the eventual presence of vertical, tightly fitted siding that offered protection from the weather.

A huge walk-in fireplace takes up most of a long wall—the outside chimney becoming a center chimney in 1791 when the size of the house was doubled by a brick addition. Within the fireplace to the right, a seat was built into the stonework, and the hooks for pots remain in good condition. The design of the fireplace indicates that the house was probably built by settlers moving out from Philadelphia. Another room was divided from the larger one, and close examination reveals a faint patched area in the middle of the interior wall, indicating a previous, smaller stone fireplace. In this room which the owners are planning to use as a library, a later corner fireplace is typical of the ones built by the Swedes in Delaware. It was probably built at the same time as the brick addition. In the room above, soot stains hint of a stone and mud chimney that was far less than airtight. In the attic, the chimney is cut off, indicating that only the large fireplace has been used for some time. Another corner fireplace appears in the brick addition. There may have been a loft over the main room in the log house, with the second floor coming along with the brick section. Pegs near the original front door could have been a ladder to the loft. Another addition, built of rubble stone (irregular pieces with some brick thrown in) was probably a separate kitchen, complete with a beehive bake oven that had a chute through which the ashes could be pushed into the fireplace for removal. Most unusually, two heavy iron pots were built permanently into the side of the kitchen fireplace.

Jim Smith, the carpenter working on the restoration, has been hand-planning new boards for replacements to match the wall boards between the two rooms. He is intrigued that the paneling is either slightly narrower at the top and wider at the bottom, or the reverse. When he removed and then replaced sections of paneling, they looked strange until he realized that he had to alternate boards of the same dimension. Someone was being creative all those years ago. There is a definite roll to the surface of the old boards, and the floors tilt noticeably. The beams are chamfered, even in the attic, showing attention to detail that is surprising for the early 18th century. Nail holes in the beams betray the existence of a plaster ceiling somewhere along the way. Were the beams chamfered in the earliest days of the log house, or was that a decorative touch somewhat later? Oddly shaped spaces were nearly impossible to identify as having a particular use and wherever possible, they have been turned into closets and cupboards.

There are remnants of porches, of openings where windows were replaced with smaller windows. Newer molding around a window follows the line of the original opening and looks unbalanced. Peg holes show up in seemingly strange places. Chinking was added where there hadn't been chinking, in response to the movement of logs. Decay accelerated by

Above: *Elijah Oliver Place, Great Smoky Mountains National Park, Gatlinburg, Tennessee*

Right: *A deserted roadhouse echoes back to pioneering days on the Alaska highway*

removal of the siding had to be dealt with—two-and-a-half inch slices of the hewn logs were cut out and replaced with equivalent slices from well-aged wood that the restorers had been collecting—the repair is referred to as a "Dutchman."

Jim Smith showed us the inventory of planks and beams stored in the shed. He and his boss, Jim Groff, pick up good materials whenever and wherever they find them and store them away for the day they are needed. Some people collect antiques, while Groff is clearly a dedicated collector of restoration projects. He feels that the key to a successful restoration is preservation of as much of the original fabric as possible—through the repair of various sections but by not tearing out, for instance, a log that requires substantial filling. A new log looks new no matter how carefully it is stained, while a semblance of grain can be scratched into the fill which will be stained to come close to the natural weathered grey. A decision had yet to be made about how to seal the outside surfaces of the

hewn logs to protect them from further decay. Some of the available sealers would darken

them to near-black, erasing the attractive weathered silver grey—and there is a difference

between indoor and outdoor sealers. Indoor sealers do not work outdoors—especially ure-

thane which decomposes.

An historian at a nearby university has a gift for the owners, a collection of research

he has developed out of fascination with this particular log house's history and progress to a

more modern home—modern being the infrastructure, heating, cooling, electricity and all the

other amenities that no one wants to see when you're thinking 18th century. My own

thoughts about the house's history may be flawed, but it certainly is fascinating to try to put

the pieces together.

CHAPTER 7

...And Present

A few miles away, over a few hills and valleys, a fifteen-year-old log home perches high on a hill, well protected as it nestles into the edge of the woods. The view from the living room is spectacular, a feeling of western space in eastern Pennsylvania. An hour's visit here is like taking a giant step all the way to Montana or Colorado. The natural setting was serendipity, but the house was the product of a nearly infinite planning exercise.

A little solitude sounded welcome to the cabin builders after years of being in the public eye, a place where they could renew spirit and energy. The land they discovered begged for a strong, solid, simple house, and that is exactly what they built.

Neither knew anything about log house construction and, it proved, neither did their chosen contractor. They would learn together. The pace of their lives dampened any thought of cutting logs on their own property. The best solution was to develop a wish list and basic design and then choose a company that specialized in pre-built log houses. Vermont Log Homes was the lucky company. The result is a wonderful, spacious, unpretentious home that feels like a vacation house—warm and welcoming.

Left: *Kantishna Roadhouse, Alaska*   **This page:** *Sled dogs and sled at Wolf Run Cabin in winter, Steese, White Mountains, Alaska*

Above: *C*abin
at Christmas, Girdwood,
Alaska

Right: *Wolf Run Cabin,*
Steese, White Mountains,
Alaska

The owners realized they had to be actively involved. Without an architect, every day brought decisions to be made. They had ideas of their own, just like the pioneers. A day never passed without a challenge. The best advice they received was to avoid major changes, and this was far more than merely avoiding the expense of changing orders. Working with regular house framing is light years away from building with logs. Log house construction becomes a matter of thinking things out in advance

Overleaf: *A remote cabin and the Aurora Borealis northern lights on a winter night*

Above: *Log cabin at the Burntside Lodge*

or living with the mistakes. It is almost impossible to go back and make adjustments. However, once the basic design was confirmed, two huge trucks arrived from Vermont, laden with random length logs that were eight inches in diameter. The log cabin was on its way.

The major elements were easy. There was agreement on a vestibule between the front door and the main room to conserve heat. It would also serve as a mud room for the dogs when they came in wet and dirty. Dutch doors for both the outside and inside doors would create a territorial limit for the dogs when necessary without excluding them. The laundry would be adjacent to the kitchen, and that worked in very well. The master bedroom and a large bath on the first floor would provide single floor living in what was actually a three story house—including a lower level made possible by the hillside site. Three small bedrooms and two baths directly over the master bedroom area are closed off when not in use. Sufficient heat flows through openings high in the main room fireplace wall to keep pipes from freezing while each second floor bedroom has its own electric heat supply when guests or family are "in house."

The enormous L-shaped main room combines the living room, dining room and kitchen with a very large, raised stone fireplace in the living room for which about two-thirds of the space is reserved. Opposite the fireplace, in the dining area, a handsome old black iron cookstove has been meticulously restored to supply heat and occasional cooking. For the grandchildren, the expansive space is an invitation to run and make noise—which they do.

Since logs are both the exterior and interior surfaces of the house, there is no room for insulation. It appears as if the logs sit directly on top of one another, but there is actually a thin strip of foam concealed between them—and no chinking. There is minimal latitude for settling or shifting in any direction.

In order to balance the expanses of dark wood, skylights were always part of the plan. Originally there were to be four of them on the south slope of the roof. The builder encouraged them to shift to two on each slope which was a good move, providing better light throughout the day.

This house was a classic case of "the devil is in the details," especially in determining how to design wiring and heating in relation to solid walls without any air spaces to run wires and pipes. The location of each pipe, outlet, and switch was chosen well before construction began. Holes had to be drilled and checked for the match with the log below or above. All the light switches would be on the interior walls that separated the vestibule, main room, laundry, and kitchen, and also in the interior walls in the bedroom wing. Some of the wiring would run under the floor and then up into the baseboards. Channels for track light wiring were drilled through the log walls and then the wires were run along the top of the heavy cross beam on which they are mounted. A superb, imaginative, patient electrician was crucial—and they found him.

The heating and cooling systems had their own set of challenges. The highest priority was to make them as inconspicuous as possible which was accomplished by running the pipes

Above: *An early settler's "root cellar," Waldron, Washington*

Right: *Coneflowers, bee balm, and bergamot in front of a log cabin*

under the floor and installing floor vents at the edges of the main room. Overhead, "Casablanca fans" (type, not brand) were planned for every bedroom, for both cooling and the circulation of heated air.

A huge laminated beam runs the length of the 24 feet x 48 feet main room to hold up the roof. Balanced on an extremely large jack, it was raised inch by inch until the ends slipped into notches on the end wall and in the massive stone chimney that were ready to receive the beam.

Every log house—dating back to the 1700s—has been subject to shrinkage. Much of the restoration effort for a really old log cabin concentrates on correcting log movement caused by the drying out process. In nearly every new log home, moisture is part of the package. In this house, the fireplace, central heating and wood stove dried the wood out over time—to the accompaniment of audible "cracks" and "pops." This is predictable behavior, experienced also by owners of custom-built timber frame houses. One reassures children and grandchildren by telling them it is the house talking to them.

CHAPTER 8

Adaptive or New Construction

There is a log cabin to suit almost any modern taste and requirement. Restoration is one option for preserving a log cabin or house on its original site, but there seems to be increasing appeal to adaptive restoration in which a log structure may be taken apart, transported to a new site, and then rebuilt with the addition of new materials and amenities. The reuse of old hand hewn logs preserves the craftsmanship of yesteryear. Timbers the size of those used in the early log cabins are hard to find for there is little virgin timber left. There are fewer species from which to choose. The historic wear and tear, expressed in bullet holes, gun ports, names and dates carved by the homesteaders, pegged ladders and soot stained beams provides an aura of those who came before—and confirms that history lives on when it is preserved. The earliest log cabins are far more apt to have pegs than nails—and the rare nails that are found bring up to $1.50 each, making them useful and attractive to hang things on but too precious to use in the building process.

Finding a good cabin to restore, or to move and rebuild, is a challenge. Many log cabins are well concealed under later additions, plank or clapboard siding, and plaster or stuc-

Left: Log working area with log cabins in the background, Fort Clatsop National Memorial, Oregon **This page:** *A man in the process of building a new log cabin*

co. The search itself is a bonus, generating opportunities to meet people, ask questions and learn more about the history of a region and in particular to gather the stories behind your potential log house purchase. Locals tend to be leery of dealers, but often respond to genuine interest with wonderful stories.

"Old" is never synonymous with "quick," and patience is an indispensable virtue. No dismantled house is ready to be reassembled without substantial repair and replacement—nor will it be a bargain. Chances are that the new owner will pay handsomely for its history as a log cabin, with the final cost about the same as using all new materials.

In shopping for an already dismantled log house, ask for a photograph taken before the dismantling began to use as a reference in looking over the stored materials. Match what you see in the photo with the components you are looking over. Bring a knowledgeable person along; it will be money well spent. A few simple tools will help determine the worth of the cabin-in-pieces: an ice pick with which to probe for rot—knotholes, cracks, and the ends of logs where they dovetail. A heavy hammer to check for a hollow sound or the rattle of rotten spots. If logs have been peeled and then exposed to the weather, they may have rotted badly. Watch too for long, lateral cracks that let water in—and tell-tale evidence of insects. Short pieces of logs are not original; they indicate repair.

It may require several old cabins to create a large enough house for a modern family. The entire operation demands careful attention and plenty of professional advice. Planning is an exercise in choosing exactly what you need—sheds, barns, granaries, another log cabin of the same era. Old round logs with bark can be hewn to make great replacement building logs since they have been protected from the weather. It's difficult to find new logs that are even close to the size of the antique ones.

Dismantling can be dangerous, especially if considering a do-it-yourself project. Step-by-step books are available, but if done correctly, this is a slow job—working from the top down, leaving the floors until last. You don't want to drop a log on your foot—or actually drop one at all. They are heavy! Experienced restoration workers will remind you to watch out for wasps' nests, snakes, and bats, too.

The size of the logs may determine the new floor plan, so the very first task on the list is to carefully measure every single log and indicate the placement of notches—a portrait of your log cabin as it stands before dismantling. Don't forget to number each piece along the way, not with magic marker or paint but with metal tags that won't wash away. Accommodation of electrical wiring, plumbing, heat, and cooling systems are major challenges that must be met while preserving as much of the original character of the construction. Not easy, but worth the effort.

A restoration effort offers opportunities for plenty of creativity, especially in thinking about insulation between the logs: Traditional chinking doesn't do the job. It becomes a matter of getting the protection from drafts and cold that you want, at the same time making everything look as if it's still an 18th or 19th century house. Things to think about include

Above: *Moose antlers decorate an antique food cache built high above ground to keep out animals*   **Right:** *Snow-covered cabin, Smoky Mountains National Park, John Oliver Place, Cades Cove, Tennessee*

Above: $\mathcal{A}$ *log cabin near Shell, Wyoming*

Overleaf: *A panoramic of a log cabin surrounded by mountains in Twin Lakes, Colorado*

whether you want a basement (yes), and the advice that the reconstruction schedule should try for mild, low-humidity weather to insure that the logs fit tightly. The little touches can be the most fun, like searching for hardware that adds authenticity, or lighting fixtures that are subtle enough to be nearly invisible.

Of course, a serious alternative is to visit one of those 240 Internet sites to research new log homes that may not look old to begin with, but will only get better with age. Contacting the companies that produce kits or modular models will fill the mailbox with catalogues and plans. Mass production means fairly obvious uniformity and lower consumer cost, trading off the uniqueness of historic log homes. Each choice has its merits, and the menu can be quite overwhelming. Allow plenty of time for considering alternatives. Naturally, the handcrafters come the closest to producing a beautifully crafted log home, but there are other good companies that supply high quality products.

Hand-hewn log homes are prepared in the traditional manner. Then the logs are cut, assembled for fit, and then disassembled and shipped to the building location. Known as pre-building, these packages can be marketed in areas where there is no natural supply of wood. However, the prospective owner had better know exactly what he wants. The log shell arrives without any extras. The on-site contractor has to put it together and also recruit subcontractors, looking for team members who understand the challenges.

Combinations of materials—sawn logs, round logs, stucco, post, and beam framing—allow nearly unlimited variety in design. Post and beam mixes well with log construction, especially in framing the roof. There is always great scope for imagination—new designs for dovetailing and notching, too. The use of naturally odd-shaped pieces of wood for stair railings and trim can be attractive, artistic and unusual. Spanish influences like stuccoed fireplaces and tiles work well within log homes. Retaining bark can be attractive, but remember, you're issuing an invitation for the bugs to come along for the party. Nothing is "wrong." Log homes take nicely to extensions.

Log homes have a history that combines appeal with practicality. Out west, where there seems to be more than the usual number of log homes, entries should be sheltered, either with an inside vestibule or at least a recessed entry. The climate suggests caution when thinking about lots of big windows which gather in the views, but the cold comes, too. Heavy snows dictate special attention to load bearing walls. As log houses expand and contract with the weather and humidity, they have been known to crack poorly placed or badly scaled windows—and also create new places for the air to creep through. Log homeowners never finish checking for air leaks. Surprisingly, log homes are not necessarily more vulnerable to fire than other structures. Flame spread has been proved to be slower because the logs are so thick. Natural wood generates less toxic fumes than houses built with space age materials.

In Closing, there is one more question. Would you like to live in a log cabin?

BIBLIOGRAPHY

Bealer, Alex W. and John O. Ellie. *The Log Cabin.* Barre Publishing, 1978

Jordan, Terry G. *American Log Buildings.* University of North Carolina Press, 1985

Lillard, Richard. *The Great Forest.* Alfred Knopf, 1948

Seton, Ernest Thompson. *Rolf in the Woods.* Grosset & Dunlap, 1911

Thiede, Arthur and Cindy Teipner. *American Log Homes.* Rodale Press, 1986

Weslager, C.A. *The Log Cabin in America: From Pioneer Days to the Present.*
    Rutgers University Press, 1969

Interviews with Jim Groff and Jim Smith, Carol Vermeil

Above: *The Hermitage, home of President Andrew Jackson, Nashville, Tennessee.*